To Nancy

Scarcity to Abundance

A 5 Step Plan

to spending your life freely

by Jennifer Mann

Thank you for coming!
20 Oct 2018

Jennifer C?

Published by Jennifer Mann

Issued in print and electronic formats.
ISBN 978-1-7751996-0-1 (pubk.)
ISBN 978-1-7751996-1-8 (ebook)

Layout and cover design: Esther Hart
www.heartsolutions.com

Personal Acknowledgements

From the bottom of my heart, I deeply and humbly appreciate the generosity of all of my clients who over 30 years shared their personal stories with me. My Write Group friends for their patient support. My husband Douglas and my parents Pam and Gil, who got enthusiastic about the idea of this book while we were all together in Hawaii. I am also thankful for all the difficult financial experiences in my life. They motivated me to form my ideas and search for a new way to live. And to Camilla, with special appreciation, who always puts her best foot forward.

'We live forward but we understand backward'
Kierkegaard

Introduction

Are you experiencing the symptoms of money "addiction"? You may be thinking about money incessantly, worrying about how to get more, and experiencing highs and lows after spending. Retirement may feel out of reach, money a source of worry and anxiety and a constant struggle. If you want your life to be more gratifying, then this book is for you.

Out of my personal financial journey and shaped by stories I heard over a span of 30 years of my counselling career, I realized that we need a new way to deal with finances, that goes beyond budgeting. This new way is to re-work how we emotionally connect to money. The 5 Step Plan will help you to change how you think, feel and behave with money. Experienced through the stories of real people, the 5 Steps come alive, showing you how to gain control of your money and your life.

Of course, no one book, or one person, has all the answers, so I encourage you to use as many resources as you need, including debt consolidation services, other books, on-line information, money coaches, bankruptcy trustees, counsellors, trusted friends and family. Don't delay if your financial situation is serious.

It's completely understandable to want change to happen quickly. Yet true change requires us to evaluate, then persevere with problem-solving *over time*. We may be very motivated at the beginning of the change process, yet no one has the drive to do what is necessary to make life-altering changes every minute of every day. Take breaks from your efforts, re-read parts of this book that energize you, or make the most sense to you. Success will be taking and integrating even one concept in this book, as one change always creates the potential for another change to occur. I appreciate your trust in buying this book and welcome your feedback and I'd love to hear about your own successes in your personal journey.

Contact me at jennifer.mann.ca@gmail.com

Contents

Chapter One:
No one is immune from the pressure to consume

The drive to accumulate money has enabled the creation of our greatest human achievements and yet accumulation also underpins some of humanity's darkest deeds.

Spending is in our social DNA. We are constantly bombarded with messages to spend, and most of us will succumb to the pressure at some point. Money controls everything in our lives. How we recreate, how we educate our children, what we eat, where we live and how we relate to one another. Stand and listen at any social gathering, and soon you will hear somebody talking about what something costs. We are obsessed with money.

If your life is like a movie, unfolding scene after scene, its tyrannical director is "money." Feelings about money are very powerful. For example, if you feel guilty about spending on yourself, you might put off important events or decisions because you don't feel "quite right" about spending on yourself. You might spend freely on others and feel good about that, or you could feel resentful and obligated to spend.

Your feelings about yourself will connect to your relationship with money and ultimately to how your life unfolds.

If you've never had an opportunity to consider this before, unknowingly the money director has created your life for you, and you haven't even agreed to the ending! If some of your feelings are similar to what has been described so far, imagine for a moment the day that you don't feel guilty, full of shame or resentful. That day will bring an experience of inner emotional freedom that will be one of the biggest highs you've ever experienced. And the money director will get a pink slip.

Every time we think about money, we feel an emotion, negative or positive. In the example that follows, the decision to spend starts with experiencing several emotions and thoughts e.g. fear of missing out, needing to belong, or wanting to have fun with friends. These feelings and thoughts become linked to how much and how readily we spend. If cycles are created, through the repetition of behaviors, thoughts hook onto emotions and begin to drive our behaviors, unbeknownst to us. When we repeat behaviors that hurt us, we can be sure that hooked up emotion and thought patterns are in the driver's seat. For example, how often do you spend, without truly *needing* to?

THE MONEY DIRECTOR IS SHOOTING, camera please ... "DINING WITH FRIENDS"

Act One

Scene One: Friends call with an invitation to dinner. They want to go to an expensive restaurant. You justify going because you feel you deserve a night out with friends.

Scene Two: Parking downtown is expensive, so you decide that you will park further away from the restaurant to save the parking fee.

Scene Three: Feeling anxious about the money in your account, you check your Visa bill before you go, hoping you are not over the max.

Scene Four: While checking the balance in your account, into your email pops a reminder about your other credit card bill. You feel heightened anxiety.

Scene Five: You tell yourself that you'll get to it tomorrow. Your shirt is OK, but since it's a nice restaurant you go to change. As you survey your wardrobe, you realize that the shirts you like are too small, your pants are a little tight, but you know that you don't have the money to buy something to wear.

Scene Six: You go out to your car, see that the gas gauge is low, but you hope you'll make it, again feeling anxiety.

All these scenes have occurred before you get to the restaurant! Money is affecting your thoughts, feelings and behavior at every juncture. At this point, it might be hard to swallow that steak which inevitably turns out tougher than you would like.

Despite what you may believe about yourself and money, we are *all* savers and *all* spenders. A tendency to be a saver or spender is simply a matter of degrees. Judgments are often made about ourselves or others when it comes to saving or spending money, as being good or bad. Yet, when factually stated, saving isn't better than spending, nor is spending any better than saving.

Whatever you feel about spending or saving, these feelings have potential power to determine outcomes in your life. In a deeper sense, your feelings about yourself will connect to your relationship with money and ultimately to how your life unfolds.

When you get paid, money appears in your bank account. What follows is a holding period, while money exists on your digital bank page. As time goes by, your life events are occurring creating the conditions for your spending. These events will trigger emotions running from positive to negative. It will be these feelings which will cause you to either spend in a restrained, or in a more impulsive manner. An internal or external event can become entrenched as a trigger to spend. Then, each time that event occurs, you have a conditioned response to that trigger, without much, if any, conscious thought.

Because of the shame attached to them, personal money difficulties are rarely openly shared. We are very familiar with addictions to drugs and alcohol, yet money is society's unacknowledged addiction. Many of us are addicted to money, either in the acquiring or spending of it. Addiction is the pursuit of something that is harmful to us, and we become compulsive in our usage. We pursue accumulation of money to our detriment and to our planet's detriment, using money for much more than simply buying the goods and services we need. We use money to cover up our feelings, and use credit to further our ability to buy, even in the face of never-ending and ballooning debt repayments. When you are struggling in your relationship to money, money rules every thought and feeling.

Sacrifices made to earn money can create imbalances that are hard to correct. These could be of your time, emotional energy, physical health, and even the overuse of money itself. We rarely realize in the moment that we are using up our valuable life hours to accumulate money. When we spend, we have to go out and earn that money again, using up more non-renewable life hours. A human version of the hamster wheel. It's understandable that we are drawn to multiple get- rich-quick schemes when we are on a conveyer belt to the weekend.

Creating a balance between consumerism and conservation of your precious resource is the essence of the 5 Step Plan. You might think that I mean money when I say precious resource. However, the most precious resource is the remaining time you have to live your life. Once used, time cannot be replenished. Changing what you spend money on and how you spend your money will change your life in extraordinary ways. No matter whether your earnings are high or low, or somewhere in between, the 5 Step Plan's evaluative process is an investment in you, which will pay you back in measurable ways such as more time, more money, more control, more freedom, more options, calmer emotions and improved physical health, as you free your mind and wallet.

Ideas about budgeting and saving *sound* good, however, these exercises fail just as many times as going on a diet does. The 5 Step Plan will take you beyond "being able to live within your means." This phrase is in common usage, yet, truthfully, very few people are living within their means. Likely not you, nor your neighbor, or your government. The desperation that ensues when there is not enough money to pay bills, eats at your soul, destroys your joy and deepens your stress. Desperation will undermine your creativity, your health and your ability to live life fully. Whatever your spiritual belief system, whatever your actual access to economic power, your everyday life is where you can and must exercise your will. Today, innumerable options are available for how we spend our leisure time, yet, money woes mean that many of those options are not available to you. By healing at a deeper level, and changing your relationship with money, you will have more control to determine your life.

To reach the final step, each step should be completed. Once you start the 5 Step Plan, you can always come back to a previous step and continue to refine your ideas. The 5 steps are simple, yet there is nothing simple about making changes, as you will see from our examples. Building new habits requires many alterations of emotions, thinking, and behavior.

5 Step Plan FAQs

"How come I can't think my way out of my money problems? I'm a rational person. I know better."

The way you think, feel and perceive has been in place for the whole of your life until today, representing thousands of hours of practice of being who you are. When we are Hungry, Angry, Lonely or Tired, (HALT), we tend to default to our old ways. Thinking, feeling and behaving differently (the holy trinity of cognitive behavioral therapy) are simple concepts, yet challenging to apply. You are a unique person. You will use the steps I present in your own unique ways. As modern life is so speedy, rarely are there moments when you can sit and think or allow yourself to do so. Our speedy life often makes us believe that changing habits developed over a life time can be speeded up too!

"Do I have to change everything about me?"

No. Not all of your spending is problematic. However, some of your thoughts may be stuck in negative cycles. These negative cycles are very familiar and ingrained, leading to familiar and ingrained responses. These are the responses that the 5 Step Plan is seeking to address.

"Are the people real in the book?"

They are and they are not. In my practice I observed that although everyone is unique, there are universal struggles within people and within families, no matter what their cultural background was. To protect confidentiality, I used those themes of concern to create each narrator. These are the kinds of struggles I heard over and over again and I hope that there will be at least one narrator that you can identify with and follow them as they navigate each Step.

"How long will it take for progress to occur?"

Some of the steps will move you forward quickly, and others will require more practice. Applying the steps will make a difference right away, as I hope you experience increasing awareness and a sense of control in your life. As you practice and integrate each Step, you may find that these ideas extend to other areas of your life.

"Is there any science behind any of these ideas?"

There is gathering evidence. For example, brain scans at Stanford University showed that just imagining that we are about to receive money, will light up the same area of the brain as sex, food, and drugs do. This suggests we are neurologically wired to become addicted to money. Research into emotions and decisions at Harvard suggests that even small amounts of emotion direct our spending. Given these findings, what would large amounts of emotion do to our spending patterns? If you'd like to read this research, the information is at the back of this book.

"What are the 5 steps?"

I use the acronym **F-L-A-R-E** which I define as 'to burn with intensity in your life, to widen your life into what you want it to be'.

Step 1: **F is for Family:** Gain understanding of how your family related to money and how that affected you.

Step 2: **L is for List:** Create the habit of listing your spending to identify spending trends.

Step 3: **A is for Awareness:** Learn how to identify your internal permission-giving statements.

Step 4: **R is for Rework:** Gain control through the

development of your motivator statements.

Step5: **E is for Experience:** Abundance is developed through your personal plan.

"How can only 5 steps actually work?"

The 5 Step Plan may sound simplistic. However, it addresses the fundamental nature of our existence; that is how we think, feel, and behave. Identifying, altering and integrating changing these fundamentals is challenging. A clear-cut plan helps to structure the changes you desire.

---

*Our emotional wounds will show up
in how we spend our money.*

Chapter Two:
Step One: F is for Family - Investigate how your family deals with money

Writing creates awareness, helping us to develop insights, and see patterns.

We become members of our society by first being inducted as members into our first exclusive club, our family. Each family has a culture of its own, with rules about how we are supposed to behave, think and feel. Our family rules for thinking, feeling, and behaving are practiced over and over again by us, whether we are aware or not aware of doing so. Rules are further entrenched by our family's unique system of reward and punishment. This part of our socialization process provides important clues as to why managing money later can be very challenging. As we mature, our executive-thinking functions develop, which when connected to our needs for approval, affects how we make our decisions. For example, if you as a child asked yourself, "Should I take this cookie?" you will have a good idea of how your Mom might react, and in response to that question, you will have had an internal emotional response based on your knowledge. This internal emotional response may occur thousands of times as you grow up. The relationship between your thoughts, feelings and behaviors develop seamlessly. Years later, you might not remember your initial emotional reaction, but you will be familiar with your behavior and choices in everyday life.

Thousands of experiences occur and re-occur in our lives, ranging from positive to negative. When experiences remind us of our previously emotionally charged events, we feel, we then analyze our feelings and then we do something or react to our feelings (whether we actually feel these emotions in the moment or not). Emotionally charged events act as triggers to our feelings, thoughts and behaviors. Triggers become ingrained and automatic.

We all have external and internal triggers to spend. And, like a trigger in a gun, once the hammer hits the firing pin, the bullet is going to explode out of the gun and head toward the target. There will be no stopping it. Our spending triggers can be more powerful than our conscious thinking, which is why I'm using a powerful metaphor to describe triggers. When our feelings are activated, the triumvirates of feeling, thought, and action are ignited chemically. We can find ourselves acting in ways that are uncomfortable but familiar. It's the familiarity and the strength of our emotional reaction that indicates the presence of a trigger.

In some families, money is scarce and there is a constant fight to acquire some. In others, money replaces parental attention. Sometimes money is talked about; other times it acts as the musical score you never see but the song you are dimly aware of playing in the background. Perhaps a sibling seemed to get more, or less than you. Innumerable money experiences shape us. We can't remember everything that happens to us, but there may be transformative money experiences that stays with us. Like the first time you got pocket money, or when you got that first paycheck. Other experiences will leave subtle traces in your consciousness. Even the experiences you don't remember leave an indelible mark on your present spending habits.

Your parents or caregivers had their own reactions to money. These were integrated into who you are through your observations and modelling. When they worried, you likely worried. When they were angry, you were likely angry, when they were fearful, you were likely fearful. Your personal story will show you what you did with that information. For example, did you become fearful, only spending when absolutely necessary? Or maybe you mimicked your caregivers, and spent to feel better?

Families often adopt common phrases to guide members' behavior with money. For example, "money isn't the most important thing," "money doesn't grow on trees," "a fool and his money are soon parted," "early to bed, early to rise, makes a man healthy, wealthy and wise," "you should always buy things on sale" and "health is better than wealth", amongst many. By the time we are adults, we are often living out the rules about how to interact with money, without much questioning of these rules. They have become who we are.

Money inhabits a special emotional space inside of us, as do all of our concepts or beliefs that make up the fabric of our lives.

Step 1 is not about spending hours criticizing or analyzing your family. Step 1 is about getting a feel for those early money influences. The following questions may help guide or prompt you. You may have strong emotional reactions to these questions. Simply notice what they are. Try not to judge yourself. Most of us feel shame, confusion or even fear about money at times. Let any shame or blame go. No matter what your early influences were, you were not in control of what messages you received about money, or about yourself. Your parents or caregivers were likely themselves unconscious about the messages they received and how they lived their lives based on those messages. Understanding what has shaped you, will help you control how you spend and why. Only write a maximum of two pages. If you need to, you can return later to write more.

1. When you were around 7 years old, did you sense or know if your parents had enough money to take care of you?

2. Did your parents or caregivers argue about money? Was there a sense of tension around money?

3. Who earned the most money in your family? Did that change over time due to unemployment, illness, or other factors?

4. Who had the power to direct spending in the family? Did that change over time?

5. Were you ever ridiculed for not having the latest or greatest?

6. Did you go without because of a lack of money?

7. Did your parents have separate or combined finances?

8. Did you hear your parents negotiate around money?

9. Were you encouraged to save?

10. What was valued in your family? Did it cost money? What were money priorities?

11. Did extended members of your family have money? Was their economic situation different to yours? How was any difference perceived in your immediate family?

12. Were there any traumatic events related to money such as separation, divorce, illness, immigration, or multiple moves?

13. Were you expected to spend any money you made on necessary consumables such as clothes and food or were you allowed to spend your money on other items?

14. Did having money imply status to you?

15. Did Mom, Dad or another caregiver complain about spending money, or spending money on you?

16. Were you worried about how the bills would be paid in your family?

17. In which areas did your parents spend on themselves?

18. Was there a prevailing sense about money being bad or good?

Before you start your personal story, Sharon, Bob, Lorna, Wendy, Mary and Carol will all share theirs. We will hear about the reasons they were seeking help and about how their families related to money. Each person uses the Steps in their own unique way. You may identify with one person more than the others. If you wish to, follow that person through to Step 5. You don't have to follow the others to gain an understanding of how the 5 Step Plan works. After reading their personal stories, you will be ready to begin Step 1.

Sharon (45)

Bio information:

Married to John for fifteen years

Mother of two

Dental Assistant

Father died when Sharon was fifteen.

Reason for seeking help: Gambling problem

Sharon called early on a Monday and left a message on my voicemail. When we talked later that day, she came across as warm and friendly. She said she wasn't in a hurry to meet; "Whatever works for you." Sharon was as warm in person as she had sounded on the phone. She was petite, mother of two, and wife to John for fifteen years. She told me that she was the kind of person that always said yes when she was asked for help. She worked hard at her job at a local dental office, helped out at her kids' hockey games, had baked a million (she was sure) cupcakes for school functions and somehow found the time to take care of her mother who wasn't well. Her father had passed away when Sharon was fifteen, and Sharon had become a confidant and helper to her mother ever since that time. To everyone else, Sharon would have appeared to be happy, engaged and fulfilled. However, Sharon had a secret, one that was eating her alive. Sharon had developed a gambling problem and was hiding that fact from John. Up until a few months prior to our initial meeting, her losses had been small, something she could hide. However, as time went on, she had begun to lose more money than she could afford. On the inside, hidden to others, Sharon was constantly anxious. On the outside, it appeared that she was competent and in control. Turning to online gambling, (where losses can accumulate rapidly), she had begun to lose amounts of money that she wasn't going to be able to hide forever. Sharon was fearful and desperate, and she knew that once the secret was out, life wasn't going to be the same.

Sharon's Family History

"I grew up in a traditional family. Dad worked, Mom stayed at home. Her way of escaping was bingo. She went every week, religiously. Nothing would come between her and her Friday night bingo! Mom had a hard childhood, growing up poor on the farm. She was expected to do everything for everyone. I think it made her a little hard. She wasn't particularly affectionate, although I knew she loved me. Dad was tired a lot. It's a big job running a farm. I tried to help as much I could. I could make him smile and that made me so happy. I wouldn't say our house was happy though, it was if we just got on with the job of living. There wasn't much money for things, but I know Mom and Dad tried hard. I felt bad for them. It did mean that we did without. I never complained. Not like my sister Sue!" Sharon grimaced. "I can't remember much tension if any about money. It wasn't spoken about. I think Mom handled the finances.

"Then overnight, things changed. Dad died. Totally unexpected. It was a heart attack. Mom was left with everything to do. We all tried to help. We didn't have much time to grieve. It was about getting on with life. Things got really hard financially. Rick, my older brother quit school, and helped out with the farm. But the farm had to go. We moved into town, into two rooms above the local store. We were cramped. I remember Sue and I fought because her things were always migrating over to my side of our tiny room. Things got better financially when my brother Steve started working.

"I didn't go to university, although I wanted to. I ended up working in the local dental office, and that's where I met John when he came in for a teeth cleaning. He's a good man, solid, dependable." Sharon bowed her head and tears were falling. "If he finds out that I've been gambling, I just don't know what he will do. I've spent money that could have gone into my children's university fund. How could I do that, after all I went through?"

Bob (57)

Bio information:

Married to Trish

Father of two

Engineer

Helps mother with living expenses

Reason for seeking help: Depression, chronic fatigue, concerns about his wife's spending

When Bob came into the office, he struck me as a warm, intelligent person, who had lost his way. Bob said that he needed help with his depression. He had been told that he has heart problems. He wasn't sleeping very well, and, felt chronically fatigued. He wasn't enjoying his job. His supervisor had told him that a co-worker had complained that Bob had become snappy at work. Bob was also concerned about his marital relationship. His wife had stayed at home with their children for several years, and although she had recently returned to work, their finances were stretched. Bob felt that his wife spent too much, but he felt powerless to alter her spending. He said his wife was more articulate than he was, and that he struggled to be heard by her. He wasn't happy with his life, knew his marriage was struggling and wanted help to figure things out.

Bob's Family History

"I grew up in a pretty chaotic family. It seemed like my Dad was always angry. I honestly can't remember much, but I do remember kids laughing at me at school because I had old hand-me-down clothes. I remember feeling stressed about that. Embarrassed, like it was my fault. Childhood was always about waiting for my Dad to come home and worrying about what mood he would be in. My mother would announce his imminent arrival home from work, and she'd look so stressed. We all knew what it meant."

Bob looked down at this point in his story, his brows

furrowed. "There was physical violence in our home. I saw my father hit my mother more than once. There was pushing and shoving, slapping and shouting. I knew Mom didn't have much money and it was always a struggle to get any from Dad. He was definitely in control. I got a job, I think when I was 10, helping out at the local grocery store moving boxes, and I'd give the money to my mother. Now that I have my own kids, I wonder if she really should have taken it from me." Bob paused and swallowed. I suspected that Bob did a lot of swallowing of uncomfortable feelings in his life.

"I still give a fair amount of money to my mother," Bob explained. "I feel badly for her because she had such a hard life with my dad. I feel stretched financially. There seems to be so many expenses! There's stuff for the children, they do so many sports, but we feel that is important. My job is pretty stressful and I'm expected to work long hours. I earn a decent amount of money but I don't think we have much savings. Trish is in charge of our finances. I'm quite concerned for the future, but my wife and I aren't that great talking about money. All I know is that there is quite a lot of spending going on, and it always seems to be for a 'good' reason. I ask Trish about it but she says, "It will all be fine." I really don't trust that, but I don't know how to talk to her."

Lorna (55)

Bio information:

Single

Two children

Consultant

Mother hospitalized, mostly absent when Lorna lived at home

Reason for seeking help: Wants to change eating patterns, concerns about children

Lorna came to see me because she wanted to work on the way she thought about food. She had gone up and down in her weight during her entire life and had a closet of what she called "my fat clothes" and "my thin clothes." She said that she was currently in the fat clothes side of her closet. Lorna had tried every diet, and was very dissatisfied with her body, which she referred to as "it." However, our conversation soon moved to her children. She acknowledged feeling resentful about their demands on her, but she also felt guilty about her resentment, a kind of catch 22. "I blame myself for how my children are doing," she said, her voice breaking. "I know I eat too much when I feel stressed." Helping her children took up most of her time, and Lorna experienced resentment, fear, and anger on a daily basis.

Lorna's Family History

"I think I was born feeling guilty for one thing or another. When it comes to my kids, I can't seem to say no! I've got more than one kid, so not being able to say no, has been expensive for me!" Lorna laughed at her own joke. Then her eyebrows drew together, her smile turned down and she turned to stare out of the window of my office. "My daughter has many emotional problems and can't seem to hold down a job, and I end up bailing her out for her rent. She has two kids, so I feel like I need to help her out. My son, Rory, is separated from his wife, and it's been terrible for him. He hardly gets to see his kids, and, is spending so much money just trying to see them. His car is old and keeps breaking down, so I've helped him. Their father and I separated when they were young, and I really think it affected the kids in bad ways. I worry about them so much.

"Before I went to school, my mother became very ill and was hospitalized for a year. After that point, she was in and out of hospital. My sister and brother came along later. When I was young, I became the housekeeper; cooking, cleaning, and taking care of my brother and sister. My dad had to work of course and he was gone long hours. When my mother was home, she didn't have much energy and I tried very hard to please her. I did get praise from my father about my helping around the house, but I don't think anyone noticed that my life as a child was fairly non-existent. The focus was on my Mom, or my brother and sister. I did feel guilty that she was ill and I wasn't. I could never make it up to her, although I tried to."

Wendy (42)

Bio information:

Single

Banker, works at least 60 hours per week

Childhood marred by tension between parents

Reason for seeking help: Anger, dissatisfied with life

Wendy's face was drawn and grey, her eyes shadowed. She explained that she'd had four long-term relationships; none of them had lasted. She felt desperately lonely, but, was finding it hard to develop a social life. Given that she usually worked at least 60 hours per week, Wendy acknowledged that she didn't have much energy left over for a social life. During our first visit, she talked about work only; how difficult it was, how the demands were unrealistic, and that her supervisor was very demanding of her. Wendy's life consisted of getting up, going to work and coming home. She rarely had the energy to make dinner. When I asked if she was able to say no and not take work home, Wendy became angry. She felt life was unfair and hard. She felt stuck in her situation and powerless to change it. Her parents and one sister lived across the country and, by all accounts, they were critical of her. Wendy said her mother was always commenting in a critical way, that Wendy didn't have a man in her life. Her sister tended to make similar critical comments. Wendy, understandably, was very unhappy and was considering antidepressant medication.

Wendy's Family History

"Dad worked away and didn't have much to do with me. Mom even told me that Dad hadn't wanted any kids. Yet they had two, me and my sister. If they didn't want any, why did they have kids? I don't know why she said that; it was so hurtful. I was left to my own devices so much growing up. I never had friends over from school or stayed over at anyone's house, so I had to amuse myself growing up. Looking back, I can see Mom was obviously unhappy with Dad, and she used me as her therapist, telling me things that I really shouldn't have heard. I don't blame her now, but if I had children, I wouldn't tell them the things Mom told me.

"When Dad did spend some time at home, you could cut the tension in our house with a knife. I could hardly wait to escape and left one night with a boy called Mark from high school. I thought it was romantic. I climbed out of my bedroom window like Juliet. All I took was a change of clothes and $20. We ran away to the next town. Mark's family was angry of course, and they used to call, convincing him to go home. What amazes me is that no one in my family came to look for me. We stayed for two weeks in a rooming house, and then Mark's parents arrived. They tried to convince me to go home, which I didn't want to do. I was going to make it on my own. Mark went home, though.

"Mom did call me eventually; I don't remember how hard she tried to get me to go home. If she did, I wouldn't have gone. I think I liked making her suffer. It's a miracle I've been able to do as well as I have. I'd like to travel, and I plan to retire, but my spending gets out of control. I'm pretty good for a while, then I find myself spending, often on things I don't really need. I've wasted a lot of money.

"It's only after I've spent the money, sometimes months afterwards, that I don't like whatever it is, and by then it's too late to take it back." Wendy looked upset. "I once bought five shirts in a row, and it felt like once I had started spending, I couldn't stop. I also like shopping in dollar stores, and mostly I'm buying stuff I don't really need. When I look at my Visa balance I am surprised at how much I've spent. It's weird because I don't feel like I'm overspending, but the evidence is in front of me.

"Sometimes I can wait to spend. I wasn't in the

habit of spending money on myself until my thirties. I was always able to put off my spending. Perhaps I am not being realistic with my needs. I think I sometimes pretend I don't have any needs, until I'm desperate, and then I can spend money on things too quickly and waste it."

Mary (61)

Bio information:

Married

Two children

Personal Assistant

Reason for seeking help: Concerns about son Harris and about marriage to Ed

Mary said she was 61, going on 71. She said she was constantly tired. Evidence of emotional burnout was in her continuous weeping during our first visit. Her primary concern was her son Harris, who had returned home and was living in her basement. Harris had been living away, but, had run out of money. As Mary spoke about Harris, it seemed that he had had many struggles. There was always, a legitimate reason. Harris needed rent money, Harris needed money for his car, Harris needed help to pay for a medical procedure. Harris was always on the phone, with a problem or two, needing money from his mother.

Mary's husband Ed, kept telling her not to give him money, but Harris became angry with Mary, and it was hard to deal with that anger. If Harris was desperate, he became verbally abusive to Mary, accusing her of one thing or another, as if she were solely to blame for his struggles. During arguments,

Harris would often tell her he couldn't carry on with life, and Mary would find herself giving him money to offset the implied threat of suicide. Harris was again living back home and not working very much. Mary was torn not only between her husband and her son, but also between guilt and fear that this situation was never going to end.

Mary's Family History

"I was the third child of a family of eight children. I suppose I was lost in the line-up. I was expected to help out with the younger kids, but I also had the older ones telling me what to do. I did a course in medical technology, and I enjoyed being away from home, having freedom. I think I had a tendency to follow along with my fellow students. I was pretty quiet.

"I was always good with money and was able to save. I got married fairly young and we had two children, one being Harris. I've always worried about Harris more. I'm not sure if it's because he reminds me of a boy at my high school that was bullied, or whether it's because his relationship with his father has been rocky. Maybe both. I try not to be in the middle of them, but I often stick up for Harris, even if I agree with Ed! I think Ed is upset with me because of that. It's affected my relationship in a negative way. Ed and Harris have gotten into some really bad fights. I'm so glad that I can talk to you about this because I would never tell anyone else about what my family is really like."

Carol (49)

Bio information:

Married

Manager

Violence in biological family and first marriage

Reason for seeking help: General unhappiness

The day was cool and cloudy when Carol came to see me. She had an imposing presence, and, was a person who appeared to know where she was going. However, there was a backstory that she rarely shared with anyone.

Carol's Family History

"I met my husband at 18, and we were married when I was 20," she said, wrinkling up her eyes as spoke. In her right hand she twirled the pen that she had used to sign the consent form. "I couldn't wait to get out of my parents' house. I was so naive back then. I really wasn't prepared for the realities of married life. I quickly became pregnant, and within four years had three children. I was constantly tired, worn out, I suppose." She looked down. "What I didn't know about Tom was that he was a violent person. He had no patience at all with the children, and you can imagine with such young children, how often things just didn't go smoothly. I suppose, looking back, I was trying to shield them as best as I could, but I still have guilt about what those children witnessed.

"When Tom got angry, which seemed to be every day, he started to hit me. At first it was shoves and name calling, but his behavior escalated. I was so ashamed, I couldn't tell anyone. I blamed myself.

And I was terrified that the children might be taken away. If he was angry at one of them, I knew I would be getting it later." As Carol spoke, the effects of domestic violence on her emotional and mental wellness were clear. "The abuse went on in and outside of the bedroom. He also controlled the money and would give me very little with which to manage the house. I was constantly stressed about money."

Carol's childhood years weren't that much different to what she experienced in her first marriage. "Of course, you might guess that I came from a family where there was violence. I saw my mother beaten and threatened. We didn't have much money, and my father controlled everything. A classic case, right? It took me ten years to leave Tom, and I was terrified for my life. I got some training through the (x) organization, and, found a job. I suppose I haven't looked back since, to be honest. I'm a manager for a moving company and I'm really happy in my job. I get to help people, and it feels good. I'm remarried now, and although I wouldn't say we are completely happy, our relationship is better than I had before. I do find myself lonely though and this is where my spending habits have gotten me into trouble."

Step 1: F is for Family. Take action and write your story.

Using the questions posed previously in this chapter as a guide, write a maximum of two pages about your family's relationship with money, and the ways in which your family's money culture has affected your own.

<u>Self-care activity after you've completed Step 1</u>

After you've written your own personal story, you may feel pain, jubilation, sadness, fear or a host of other emotions. Whatever you feel in the moment, simply notice. If the feelings linger, write them down. Sometimes the act of acknowledging the emotion we are feeling will reduce its intensity.

Stand up, stretch, and breathe deeply. Shake off tension. Listen to and trust yourself. Take a break outside if possible to ground yourself in nature.

Chapter Three:
Step 2: L is for List - Track your spending

When you track your spending, you are learning how to identify your problematic spending trends in Step 2.

There is always a reason for problematic spending; it does not happen in isolation from your everyday life. Your personal story will have uncovered information for you to examine. You may be aware, for example, that you buy chocolate to treat yourself when you are feeling down. The feeling afterwards should be one of happiness, yet you are also aware that you don't really feel better, or happier, but you feel compelled to keep buying the chocolate in the hopes that you will.

We are always trying to heal.

Habitual, ritualized behaviors directed by our emotional pain, just don't have healing power. However, we often believe they do and our experience *seems* to back up our belief. An example of this could be someone who constantly does things for others to feel needed, but never receives the acknowledgement they really require to heal the deeper wound. On a larger scale, our society is caught up in spending money to heal, yet, spending which derives from our emotional wounds will simply continue to wound us.

To truly heal, we have to get our feelings to work for us, rather than against us.

How and what you spend money on is revealing. Tracking what you spend will provide you with information about your emotional wounds. Tracking also manifests your belief system to you, representing who believe you are. If you spend money on golf clubs, and, are prepared to spend whatever the price tag says, well, that says something about you. If you insist on getting a haircut with all the frills then that says something too. If you take a look at your Visa bill, and you see multiple dinners out, that says something. If you restrict yourself in your spending on things you actually need, although you can afford them, then that spending trend says something also. By examining your own spending trends, you will find out what they truly mean in the context of your life.

Examining your behavioral choices around money will provide some ideas of what emotional needs are or not being met.

If the way we spend reflects our emotional wounds, paying attention to how we spend gives us excellent information about where we need to heal.

As you compile your spending list, take a look at the following list of universal problematic spending types. Your own problematic spending may fit into one or more than one type.

Impulse spending: *Wanting to buy something, with little regard to monthly deposits, bills or other outstanding debts.*

Diet spending: *Abstaining from spending for a period of time, and then finding it difficult to stop after starting again.*

Frozen frugality: *Afraid of spending, of not having enough money.*

Obligation spending: *Spending on friends or family with a sense of duty or guilt underlying the spending.*

Entitled spending: *The feeling that we should be able to buy whatever we want, whenever we want to.*

Fearful spending: *Buying multiples of things on sale, beyond needs.*

Revenge spending: *Similar to entitled, revenge when a person wants to get back at a significant other, or, spends as a result of experiencing anger towards someone.*

Angry spending: *Similar to revenge, spending when angry about something, a kind of "so what?"*

Guilt spending: *Spending on others out of feeling guilty for having money, and the impossibility of saying no in the face of requests for money.*

Step 2: L is for List. Take Action and start your list.

Keep a list of what you spend. Use pen and paper.

Text alerts, spreadsheets and apps can help us keep track; but there's no beating the simple pen and paper technique. Technology just speeds us up without helping us to integrate any new insights. We also have a tendency to forget when the information is not in front of us and all our information is tucked away in digital files. We then have to make a conscious effort to access the file on a regular basis. To develop the practice of awareness, keep the piece of paper where you will regularly see it. Work towards noting your spending every day.

Get a receipt for everything you buy, no matter how small. Keep a list of what you buy and the date of each purchase. Or take your bank statements and review them if you spend only by credit or debit.

Don't judge what you see. If you resist keeping a list imagine you are keeping the list for someone else.

Becoming an observer rather than a critic of your life is a very useful healing tool. Developing an empathic, slightly detached approach will be useful in not only changing spending habits and but also in changing other parts of your life, which may be weighing down on you.

Remain curious about the details of your life. For example, you will see how many take-outs you have, and what kind. What kind of clothes you buy, and when. A buying type will start to emerge. For example, you may notice that you tend to buy take-outs at the end of a busy week, when you are tired and needing a treat.

Once you've kept your list for a month, you will notice that there are areas in which you spend up to a limit, and rarely overspend. There will also be areas in which you regularly overspend, and those are the areas that you will be focusing on in Step 3.

Put a "p" for problematic next to the spending totals that you have some concerns or questions about. Some of your expenses are 'ok', and you can note them as such. If you add up your ok expenses, but have questions about the amount, you can also put the amount on the problematic side of the table. If you'd like a guide to how to do this, turn the page to Sharon who will be first to share her list. Sharon had expenses that she deemed ok and problematic at the same time. Items on the ok spending side of the table have been shortened for brevity. Once listed, Sharon then identified each problematic spending type.

To help identify problematic spending, ask yourself what you feel when you buy the item on the problematic spending list.

Sharon

This exercise was very challenging for Sharon. She balked at my request every time. For a person with problematic gambling issues, one of the hardest tasks is to revisit losses. I wasn't asking her to track those into the past, but Sharon carried a large amount of guilt, which guided many of her actions. In sessions, she avoided talking about what she really needed to talk about because of that guilt.

Time and empathy were needed to assist Sharon to feel less guilty and more able to open up.

Sharon tended to catastrophize her gambling, as if her actions were akin to murder. Sharon needed to detach emotionally from her actions; judging herself harshly had the opposite effect to helping her gain perspective. The larger picture of her life, or the context, was that Sharon was a generous person, who supported her family in so many ways. She needed to see that. To understand the context of your behavior(s) in your life is an effective tool. An expenditure list helped Sharon (after much prodding) to gain awareness of how her spending contributed to increasing stress and that she had the power to alter the amount of stress.

Sharon was not surprised when gambling showed up on her problematic list. Her curiosity was piqued however when we put two items on both the ok list and the problematic list. When Sharon considered her true feelings when she spent money on those items, she learned that what she had previously thought was ok spending, was actually creating problems in her life.

Sharon's List - Per Month

OK Spending		Problematic Spending		Type
Mortgage	2312	Camping and visits to Family	800	Obligation
Hydro	223	Casino Gambling	300-500	Impulse
Groceries	855	Lotteries	25	Impulse
LOC	366	Line of Credit (LOC)	366	Obligation
Camping/ visits	800			
Gambling	300-500			

"I had no idea that the trips we take add up to so much!" Sharon said. "I knew that we prioritized seeing family, and spending time as a family, but I really thought that we were being careful about how much we spent. We camp and drive, travel by air twice a year, pack picnics, buy second hand, attempting to keep the costs down. My husband really believes in family trips. When he was a boy, his family never got it together to go away. So now he wants to go away all the time."

Here Sharon paused, and gazed out of the window of my counselling office for a moment. "Truthfully, I am tired from the amount of travelling we do. With one thing or another, I never get to rest. What with the boys, my husband, my mother, my job, my friends, it's so much energy going out and not much coming in. And it's mostly up to me to get the boys ready. Don't get me wrong, I enjoy being with family, but it's so tiring."

Like many women of her age, Sharon was starting to experience some burnout from the expectations others placed on her. Yet Sharon considered them *normal* and things she *should* do. She hadn't ever considered whether these expectations were enhancing her life. Sharon never took a day off from her obligations. The only time she had to herself was when she went to the casino, which intensified her need to go.

In her detailed list, Sharon took time to consider all the expenses that made up a trip. They were many expenses such as maintenance of the trailer, insurance, buying replacement camping items, special food, arranging for care for her mother, time away from work, pet-sitters, camping sites, wood, and hiking boots. Then there were trips to see extended family. Sharon felt obligated to travel to family, although she said they had never travelled to her. Sharon had some solid justifications for why her family hadn't ever travelled to visit her. Again, the justifications were extensive such as they were busy, they had children, they were struggling financially, and they didn't like travelling. Sharon had never questioned why she burdened herself with the expenses of these trips *until she'd had a chance to question her spending.*

"I always wanted to be close to my family, but honestly, it's me that makes the effort. My sister is always talking about coming out to visit, but never does. I usually take my mother with me, but I end up paying for her so she can see her daughter."

Sharon was not happy about how large their line of credit was and that she and her husband had borrowed on the line of credit for recent house renovations. She now wondered whether all those renovations had been necessary, or whether she had been convinced so by her husband. He had wanted a large workshop, which had ended up costing more than $25,000, way over their budget which then increased their line of credit. Her husband had also wanted to start his own business, and, had bought a special machine to re-tool lawn mowers. Except the machine now quietly sat in the specially built workshop, and her husband seemed to have lost interest. "I'm quite angry with him about this," Sharon said. "What a waste of money. Every time I try to talk to him about it, he pooh-poohs my concerns and tells me he's working on his business plan. But I don't see any progress." Sharon said.

"Do you think your gambling has anything to do with how you feel about your husband spending the money on the workshop?" I asked. Sharon didn't say yes immediately, but, considered the question.

After a long pause, Sharon nodded. "My husband is a bit of a dreamer and I want to support him. And I actually feel angry with him about this waste of money. It means that I have to take extra shifts when I don't want to."

Sharon was developing a wider view of her life and the interrelationships between what she felt and how she acted.

"Sometimes I go gambling because I am angry with him, disappointed I suppose, and I just want time to myself."

Sharon ruefully acknowledged that she spent more when she went gambling when she was angry. Sometimes she stayed longer at the casino than she intended because she didn't want to go home. These actions were creating the opportunity for problematic gambling to take hold. Anger, burnout, resentment, physical tiredness and financial stress were all taking Sharon to the casino, yet those casino visits didn't solve those feelings and worries.

Sometimes we believe that we are doing everything we can, and feel frustrated with the outcome, but, if the problem is not solved, then our actions are not assisting us. Sharon was called upon to deal with her feelings differently, if she wanted to experience real change in her life.

Any action we take, that is not directed clearly at the root causes of the problem, will have no positive effect on the problem whatever the problem actually is.

Bob

As Bob was not initially involved in the family finances, he needed support and a long time-frame to sit down with his wife and start to understand the family spending.

Bob's wife, Trish, had always been in charge of the family's expenses. Bob was well aware that he was constantly trying to be the exact opposite of his father. He wanted to be the epitome of carefree and easy going. To avoid conflict, he had paid very little attention to where his money was going, and most importantly he never spoke up. Any questioning he did was silent, and he made assumptions that he never checked out with Trish for fear of creating conflict.

At the core of Bob and Trish's belief system was the importance of family. Trish gave money to her brother regularly. He struggled with a drug problem and she felt guilty about her good fortune. Trish also paid for many expenses for Bob's mother. Although Bob and Trish had both agreed to helping his mother years earlier, Bob never re-examined this choice, or examined his motivation.

Making enough money to help family and extended family put pressure on him. In tracking their spending, they realized that there were unrecognized ancillary costs. Like the food he and Trish often dropped off and taking unpaid time off work to drive his mother to her appointments. He believed this to be his duty. When we started to discuss all that he did, Bob acknowledged that he was trying to make up for his mother's difficult life, and he had not questioned this behavior. Despite all that Bob and Trish did, his mother often complained and had come to expect the sacrifices that Bob was making for her.

We might believe that we are doing the right thing by spending to make someone happy but are we really?

39

Bob's List - Per Month

Bob was shocked when the total cost for family clothing was revealed by his tracking, when he hadn't bought anything for himself for years.

OK Spending		Problematic Spending		Type
Mortgage	1652	Assisting Mother	1500	Obligation
Medical	350	Clothes	800	Obligation
Groceries	950	Alcohol	600	Impulse/ Entitled
Extras	450			
Gas	256			
Clothes	800			
Assisting Mother	1500			
Alcohol	600			

Imagining negotiating change was terrifying for Bob. Conflict resolution was a skill that Bob had not developed, nor did he have any idea of how or even if he really wanted to change. What Bob desired, was to wake up the next morning and for everything to change magically, without him having any conflict with his loved ones. "I realize now that not only did I not learn to be assertive, but I actually became the opposite of assertive, mostly passive. I tried never to upset anyone," he said, "but I am so stressed with financial demands. I love my family, but if I never say no, then surely that isn't good for them or for me?"

Lorna

Much of Lorna's overspending was for her children. Just as one crisis appeared to be over, another one would occur. Lorna had never added up the amount of money that she gave to her children. She was astounded to realize that her gifts to them averaged $1200 per month. Given that Lorna was on a fixed income, she used money from her line of credit, so the money she gave to her children was costing her interest as well. Her line of credit balance kept increasing and Lorna was having difficulty making those payments.

Lorna took her parenting role very seriously. She blamed herself almost entirely for her children's difficulties. She felt guilty about their lives, which affected her spending decisions. Her children were able to stimulate that guilt by how and what they said to her. For example, her son often told her that his life was not working out and that was her fault. After Lorna became upset, he would then ask her for money.

Breaking the cycle of blame, hurt and guilt can be very challenging.

Lorna's list - per month

I asked Lorna to include Food and Clothing on the problematic list, as these amounts seemed insufficient in comparison to the amounts Lorna provided to her son and daughter.

OK Spending		Problematic Spending		Type
Rent	800	Rory (son)	800	Angry/ Obligation/ Guilt
Utilities	250	Liesa (daughter)	500	Angry/ Obligation/ Guilt
Medical	250	Food	250	Frozen Frugality
Food	250	Clothing	50	Frozen Frugality
Clothing	50			
Rory	800			
Liesa	500			

Wendy

Wendy already had a good idea that her spending habits were impulsive, but, as a very logical person, she found it challenging to accept that there was a link between her emotions and her spending. Like most of us, Wendy assumed she was in charge of her emotions. As she tracked her spending, Wendy could see that some months she wasn't impulsive at all. Overspending on clothing, household goods, and dollar-store items appeared to come in waves, ballooning in one month and shrinking in another. We talked about what might be happening during the extra spending times to create the conditions for impulsivity.

"In January, I had two big fights with my mother and sister. They wanted me to go out for my niece's birthday. When I said I couldn't, because of work, they tried to guilt me out. They just don't understand that I have to negotiate time off carefully, as my boss can be very difficult. Then two women at work got engaged, one is pregnant and I had to attend work parties for that. I couldn't help myself, but on the way home, I stopped at the dollar store and bought a bunch of stuff. The next day I went straight to X and bought a skirt, pants and a jacket, none of which I really liked, and the spending just went on. I had no idea how angry I was."

Here I interjected, "You were probably hurt?"

Wendy looked down, tears streaming down her cheeks. "Yes, I was so hurt, so alone. I have no one in my life, and I probably never will." The pain was palpable. Wendy was making those important links between her spending and her emotions. Painful though this process was, Wendy's growing awareness was going to assist her in making different choices. Feeling alone and misunderstood in the world is extremely painful, but Wendy also believed that her state was permanent. It was going to be my job to convince her otherwise.

Wendy's List - Per Month

OK Spending		Problematic Spending		Type
Rent	950	Thrift stores	100	Impulse
Food	350	Clothes	400	Impulse/ Entitled
Transport	200	Shoes	200	Impulse
Car	150			
Shoes	200			
Thrift store	100			
Clothes	400			

Mary

Mary's confidence in her parenting of Harris had been challenged many times over the years. Friends and family criticized her. "A mother knows her children!" Mary said strongly when I began to gently discuss Harris, "and I've done my best!" Tears flowed down Mary's cheeks. Her eyes were hollowed, and she looked like she hadn't slept. In Mary's opinion, her husband Ed had always been too hard on Harris.

Harris became a lightning rod for their squabbles. Ed told her that she babied Harris and that he would turn out badly. The truth had long been obscured by fights, arguments, criticism and defensiveness. Even Mary's sister constantly told Mary that she needed to change her parenting with Harris. "She's always been bossy," said Mary, "even when we were children."

Mary was also defensive with me, no matter how carefully I discussed her situation with her. I had to support her decisions and listen closely, while I teased apart some of the faulty thinking that Mary needed to address. Her support of Harris was putting Mary in financial and emotional danger. She was spending her money beyond what she could afford, and, she was using up her emotional energy without any end in sight.

Initially Mary focused on what I might be able to offer her to help motivate Harris, or, help her deal with his anger. One of the strategies I used to move her attention from him and back onto her, was to ask her to list her extra expenses for herself and Harris for one month.

Mary's List - Per Month

Mary		Harris		Type
Lunch with Sister	25	Cigarettes	300	Angry
		Gas	50	Obligation/Guilt
		Movie	30	Obligation/Guilt
		Extras	20	Obligation/Guilt

In addition, Mary had expenses related to Harris living in her house which she hadn't paid attention to before namely:

		Hydro	200	
		Food	250	
		Medical	100	
		Upgrading	50	
		School Books	100	
		Paint for Suite	75	
		Labor	250	

When Step 2 was completed, Mary was able to see a fuller picture of her life. She became aware that in addition to money she directly provided to Harris, she was also funding his living through her house expenses. She began to take notice of another cost: the on-going relationship distress with her husband and sister.

On a deeper level, Mary felt very guilty about how Harris had turned out. She blamed herself totally for his current life, and because of that, was unable to give him the responsibility for his own life. She spent her life feeling guilty, and then hurt at how people viewed Harris and her parenting. She also believed that her other child was untouched by her focus on Harris. "I never have to worry about Chloe," Mary said, "she is able to take care of herself."

Although Mary believed this wholeheartedly, I doubted that Chloe was happy. Chloe, it appeared, had very little to do with her family, and Mary seemed oblivious to how the obsession with Harris may have affected her relationship with her daughter.

A therapist's job is to create a safe space within which clients do not feel judged. They are already judging themselves harshly, and, may be receiving criticisms from others. Over the next several months, Mary started to relax in our conversations, as she realized that she didn't have to defend her actions to me. This enabled her to look at her relationship with Harris. When she was able to look at the list of expenditures for Harris without the film of pain that often accompanies growing awareness, Mary was shocked to see how much money she was spending on Harris. Guilt, hurt and anger had promoted a sense of obligation and duty to Harris that went far beyond what he truly needed and what Mary could afford.

Carol

Step 2 helped Carol to ask new questions of herself and to see the bigger picture of her life. As Carol reviewed her spending list, she became aware that she was often late for work, which meant she missed the bus and had to take her car. This

47

increased her gas and parking spending. Running
late also meant that she didn't have time to make
her lunch, so there was spending on lunches. It
wasn't that Carol wasn't aware of her lunches out;
she hadn't had an opportunity to view this practice
in a clear way. The review helped Carol to set her
alarm at an earlier hour to ensure she had enough
time to complete her morning tasks.

Carol's List - Per Month

OK Spending		Problematic Spending		Type
Groceries	800	Chocolate	25	Impulse
Car gas	200	Shoes	75	Revenge
Insurance	25	Lunches	150	Entitled
Rent	1200	Gifts	50	Obligation
Medical	120	Dollar Store Sales	50	Impulse
Car	25	Car gas	200	Entitled
Glasses	150	Groceries	800	Guilt
		TOTAL	1350	

While Carol was musing aloud about which
categories her spending fell into, I asked her which
emotions she thought were directing her spending.
Carol drew her mouth together in a grimace and
raised her eyes slightly upward. "I would say
resentment," she said, tapping her index finger on
the arm of the chair. "I spent, no pun intended,

most of my childhood and early adulthood asking for very little for me, so I tell myself that it's my time now to spend a little on me. I didn't realize that I was spending more than a little," Carol smiled ruefully.

Other links between emotions and actions began to emerge. "When I was a child I'd hide food, otherwise sometimes I'd go hungry," she said, "and this has morphed into holding backing information from my husband; I just don't share with him. A way to have control I suppose," Carol shrugged. There was a moment of silence while Carol collected her thoughts, and her brows knitted together. "You know I think I resent my husband," she said, shaking her head. "He's a great one for lecturing me on saving my money, but, he doesn't seem to worry about how much he spends on his hobbies. From the start we've kept our money separate."

Carol's insights were coming thick and fast now. "Here I am, ready to work less, but I really can't afford it. And he spends money like water, but, doesn't offer to help me out." Carol's face was set, her eyes flashing. I was sure Carol was angry, although I try not to make assumptions. Not everyone expresses emotions in expected, standard ways. Many of us need practice in labelling our emotions correctly and expressing them. "Is that anger you are experiencing?" I asked.

She nodded. "Wow, I didn't know I was feeling so strongly about my husband." As anger settled and calmed within her, I was able to ask Carol if there was anything else she needed to do with her anger. "If anger and resentment lie underneath your spending, is there something else you could do with

49

those feelings?" I asked. The 5 Step Plan requires that people to address emotions so that they don't go 'underground' and begin to direct people's lives.

Carol was afraid of bringing up the topic of money with her husband. She was also terrified of rejection, something she had experienced many times over in her childhood. So, anger and fear were emotions which directed her Entitled Spending. Spending did not relieve her feelings. Resentment continued to build, creating a feedback loop between resentment, fear, spending, then back to resentment. Carol was *spending* her *feelings*, without ever experiencing a sense of resolution of them.

Self-care activity during and after completion of Step 2 and all Steps.

Celebrate your growing awareness by noting your insights in a journal with large letters and colorful print. Whenever you find your enthusiasm beginning to wane, you can renew and refresh yourself by re-reading your successes, changes, decisions, and insights.

Chapter Four:
Step 3: A is for Awareness -
Identifying Permission-Giving statements

Permission-giving statements are those repetitive, familiar rationalizations that propel us to actions. Their role is to prop up our decisions. We emotionally 'agree' with how we justify our actions, and they become part of our regular inner dialogue. We have a set of permission-giving statements for every facet of our lives. When it comes to money, and spending, you may have several.

Here are general permission-giving statements about money you may have heard or even use yourself.

- "I deserve to buy X."

- "I work hard, (my life is hard) why shouldn't I spend X?"

- "My_____ (fill in blank) is important/vital/crucial to my life. I can't give it up."

- "It's such a deal!"
- "If I don't buy this now, I'll never have it."
- "I have to spend X on Y, that's just the way it is."
- "There's no going back now."

Here are some general permission-giving statements about credit. Perhaps you will recognize them.

- "I'll never be able to save, so I might as well spend money on what I want now."
- "Everyone uses credit, it's part of life."
- "Being in debt is part of life."
- "Everyone I know uses credit."
- "I can pay the minimum and everything will be fine."
- "I'll pay it off next month."
- "Who can save and have enough money without using credit?"

Step 3 begins by neutrally observing your spending in the problematic area that you identified in Step 2. Then, next to each area you previously identified, write down the phrase you use to give yourself permission to spend. You could find that you have more than one reason per overspending area.

Permission-giving statements are not all bad, all of the time. They enable us to try new things, take risks, learn tasks and challenge ourselves. They can have good power in our lives. However, they come with a double edge, and they can cut. Used sparingly, permission-giving statements can motivate us, however, if we are unaware of our permission-giving statements, then they have the power to control our choices in harmful ways.

If you don't identify *all* your permission-giving statements for each problematic spending area, they will continue to direct your behavior, and the real changes you are seeking will be blocked.

How to Identify Permission-Giving Statements:

1. Start by stating the factual behavior you observe yourself repeating in one of your identified problematic categories, then find the statement that *seems* to keep the behavior going. The spending behaviors are then stated as *factually* as you can make them. For example, if you overspend on haircuts, a stated behavior may be, "I spend 50-200 dollars per haircut at least 8 times a year."

2. After you've written down the factual statement, ask yourself what you say to yourself when you are about to act. For example, I spend 50-200 dollars per haircut at least 8 times per year, **because** ...

"My hair is really difficult to manage and I need the XY treatment."

Figuring out what you tell yourself to make these behaviors possible, can be emotionally painful. Be compassionate with yourself. These reasons are deeply embedded in your thinking and it can take several attempts to be able to write them down and review them.

Sharon's Problematic Spending List

Sharon had identified the following as problematic in Step 2.

Camping and Visits to Family	1200	Obligation
Casino Gambling	300-500	Impulse/Revenge
Lotteries	25	Impulse/Revenge
Line of Credit	300	Obligation

After considering each and noting how she felt in each situation, she came up with the following factual statements about her behavior.

Sharon's Factual Statements

"I gamble when I want to, without paying attention to what I am spending."

"I go on at least four camping trips a year and two cross country trips to visit family."

"We use our line of credit to finance our trips."

Sharon's Permission-Giving Statements

I gamble when I want to **because** "The only thing that is mine is my gambling, so why should I stop?"

I go on at least four camping trips **because** "Family is the most important thing in life and I go to see them even if don't want to because that is my duty."

We use our line of credit **because** "We put our travels on our line of credit, because family is important, so we shouldn't question the amount."

Although we are rational beings, we can't forget that our rationality is imbued with our emotions, and the two comprise our humanity. We cannot heal one without healing the other. Many tell themselves, "I should have known," yet our rational thinking brain is only one part of the equation.

Step 3 enabled Sharon to see that she believed that she "only had gambling" in her life, and that she told herself she had to go on camping trips. Although uncomfortable with using their line of credit, Sharon told herself to agree to the spending, overcoming her true feelings. Resentment, anger increased, and were not expressed. Those emotions emerged in gambling. Sharon's permission-giving statements were connected to her childhood, where making her father happy was what Sharon tried to do. Money wasn't discussed at home; the thread of constant tension about money was communicated nonetheless. Sharon also learned not to complain and to become her mother's helper. We are highly influenced by how our parents deal with stress. Since Sharon's mother used Bingo to deal with stress, it's not unusual that Sharon sought out gambling as a relief from her own stress. Given that Sharon had witnessed very little communication between her parents to problem-solve, Sharon hadn't learned how to negotiate or be assertive with her own needs.

Bob

Bob believed that he alone, was responsible for his mother's happiness, and that he had to be 'nice' in his dealings with friends and family. He was aware that he was stressed, but, had not considered his spending on alcohol to be related. Drinking was something he just did when he returned from work.

Bob's Problematic Spending List

Assisting Mother	1500	Obligation/Guilt
Clothes	800	Obligation/Fearful/Guilt
Alcohol	600	Impulse

Bob's Factual Statements

"I don't question where and how much money is spent, especially on my mother."

"The only money I spend on myself is for alcohol."

"I will go along or not question too much what my wife spends."

Bob's Permission-Giving Statements

I don't question where money is spent *because* "I have to take care of my mother. My father didn't, and she relies on me."

I don't question what my wife spends *because* "I have to provide whatever my family needs, it's my role."

I spend money on alcohol *because* "I need something to relax with, I've got a stressful life."

I don't question where money is spent *because* "I must always be nice to everyone, as my father wasn't."

Bob was surprised to learn that he had permission-giving statements. He had not realized that he gave himself reasons for what he did. He practiced saying them out loud in our sessions together, and by his internal reaction, could see how powerfully they had directed his behavior in most aspects of his life.

Lorna
Lorna's Problematic Spending List

Rory (son)	500-800	Angry/Obligation/Guilt
Liesa (daughter)	250-500	Angry/Obligation/Guilt
Food	250	Frozen Frugality
Clothing	50	Frozen Frugality

Lorna's Factual Statements

"I don'l spend very much on myself in the clothing or food department."

"I often help my children out financially."

"I never say no if my children ask for help."

"I will give to my children, even if I want to save the money for my retirement."

"I give money to my children if I perceive they are struggling."

Lorna's Permission-Giving Statements

I will give money to my child *because* "Liesa needs my help, she is unable to take care of herself."

I never say no *because* "I am responsible for the way Rory's life has turned out."

I never say no *because* "A mother should always be there for her children."

I will give to my children *because* "I should spend less on myself so there is more for my children."

I will give money to my child *because* "My future retirement isn't as important as what my children need."

It took time for Lorna to re-state her problematic spending neutrally. Judgments of herself got in the way. In sessions, Lorna would revert to her old statements about helping her children. If she reported a crisis with one of her children, the old way of thinking took over. She believed that she was duty bound to help her children. Certainly, there are times to help, yet Lorna had never questioned this behavior in a neutral fashion. "What if," I asked in one session, "you said yes sometimes and no sometimes? So that when a situation was dire, you helped and when it wasn't you experimented by saying no." Lorna was stuck thinking that every situation her children faced warranted her solutions, whether it be money, or any of the other kinds of help she offered, from dinners to child-minding. In myriad ways, Lorna's valuable life energy was being subsumed by the on-going demands of her children.

Staying neutral in observation can lead to insights about how money connects to other issues. Lorna wrote out her list as best she could and then put it away, so that she wouldn't begin to argue with herself or judge what she had written. Reviewing her list multiple times was important to assist Lorna to become more neutral. There were valid reasons why she had developed her previous spending behaviors. Now, given her financial situation, and that she wanted to retire in the future, Lorna was at last looking at the biggest drain on her finances and future happiness. Parenting directed by guilt is challenging to deal with, and change was going to take time. By completing Step 3, Lorna had given herself a chance to gain control.

Wendy

Wendy had spent much of her life on her own, working out life's problems, doing the best she could. Without positive support, Wendy had not experienced a sense of self-love. A pervading sense of being unlovable, showed up in her spending behaviors and her statements list.

Wendy's Factual Statements

"I overspend money on items I don't really need."

"I overspend when I'm feeling depressed."

"I overspend after events where I'm hurt."

"I overspend in waves."

Wendy's Permission-Giving Statements

I overspend when I'm feeling depressed *because* "I only have spending to comfort me when I have negative emotions."

I overspend when I'm feeling depressed *because* "I'm caught in a lonely life from which there is no escape until I spend."

I overspend in waves *because* "I don't really care how much I spend at these times, because no one cares about me."

When Wendy shared her work with me, she experienced a paroxysm of grief. It was hard to witness the extent of her pain. We suffer both for experiences that happen to us, and for the experiences that we create based on our early learning.

Time spent in compassionate self-reflection, by acknowledging hardships and by congratulating ourselves for overcoming those hardships is a significant on-going part of the healing process.

Mary

Mary was resistant to writing down her behaviors around money. Mary's resistance to Step 3, resembled many other aspects of her life. Mary had been conditioned over time to respond in rigid ways to other peoples' suggestions as she had had to defend her actions so many times. With time and gentle persuasion, eventually Mary was prepared to try. The turning point for Mary was when she realized how many times she had resisted my suggestion(s). She acknowledged that she tended to say no (in her mind) to the ideas of others, without giving them a chance. Also, she tended to try to work problems out on her own, without asking for help.

Mary's Factual Statements

"I give money to Harris whenever he asks for it, whatever he wants it for."

"I spend my savings on Harris."

"I don't buy things I want for myself in case Harris needs something."

"I don't take advice when it comes to my money."

"My husband and I fight about the money I give to Harris."

Once Mary saw these behaviors in black and white, she wanted to immediately change them!

Mary's Permission-Giving Statements

I spend my savings on Harris **because** "I am always right when it comes to Harris and what he needs, no one else understands."

I don't buy for myself **because** "I am not as important; my son is all important."

I don't take advice **because** "If I keep trying, I'll find the magic answer to Harris' problems."

Being at heart a practical person, Mary couldn't wait to begin changing her permission-giving statements to motivators (Step 4). Working through to Step 3, hard as that the process had been, was significant. She now had the power to alter her behavior and her life.

Carol

Carol acknowledged that she liked the finer things of life; however, her ability to buy those finer things was hampered by the fact that she also overspent when she felt down, or lonely, or sad. She had a longstanding habit of not paying attention to the amounts of those shopping receipts, so didn't have a comprehensive idea of how much she actually spent. Given that she was in charge of the family finances, the problem of overspending had been hidden, as she constantly moved money from her line of credit to her credit cards and then back again. Thus far, her husband had been content to let her handle their affairs. Carol's debt load was $345,000; half being their line of credit. This amount of debt was at odds with her husband's desire to retire in the next 5 years; it didn't look possible. Carol avoided any real discussion with him, and had many sleepless nights, anxious and worried thoughts, and suffered physical problems. She and her husband lived in a state of separateness, eroding their intimate life.

Carol's Factual Statements

"I shop when I'm lonely, sad and down."

"I manage debt by moving money between credit cards and accounts."

"I'm often anxious about money and think about it constantly."

"I keep my negative thoughts to myself."

Carol's Permission-Giving Statements

I keep my negative thoughts to myself **because** "I have to keep my negative feelings to myself, no one is interested or cares."

I keep my negative thoughts to myself **because** "My spouse wouldn't love me if he knew how bad I am."

I keep my negative thoughts to myself **because** "I can't ask for help, it puts a strain on others."

I manage debt **because** "Debt is a part of life."

"I'm shocked," Carol said when we wrote these down together. "They are what I've said to myself for years!" Carol's voice broke, and tears flooded down at the realization that her life was scripted by what had essentially been hidden from her. We all respond to events in our lives and develop our habitual behaviors as a result of that internal response. Often, we need to protect ourselves or to take care of ourselves. For example, if we didn't feel particularly safe in our families, then our behavior will reflect that experience. We may not trust others to be there for us, or ask for help when we need it, which was the case for Carol. However, just as permission-giving statements may have once ruled your life, new behaviors and using motivating statements can and will alter your life in amazing ways.

Self-care activity after Step 3.

You have been working very hard to change your life. Now give yourself permission to do something fun! Some fun things may be: dancing to music, going for a walk, listening to a podcast, going to a movie, or even cleaning your cupboards. A sense of fun, creativity and lightness can be found in almost every task we do.

Chapter Five:
Step 4: R is for Re-Work -
Alter your Permission-Giving Statements into Motivators for Change

We all need strong reasons to change. Even more importantly, we need reminders of the change that we are seeking. So, your new Motivator statements will be your reminders, to help keep you on track. Think of them as powerful affirmations. Affirmations take time to work, so find time to practice saying them, or reading them through every day.

As you re-work your permission-giving into motivator statements be aware that you are developing an inner thinking space that is

1. Compassionate towards yourself

2. Without judgment and

3. Affirming.

As you may have experienced in Step 3, you may

need to revisit Step 4 many times. Your brain will resist the new motivators and initially you will want to default to the permission-giving statement. To find a motivator that resonates with you, play around with words, change their order, and don't be afraid to try out some new words, and eventually, a new statement will emerge on paper. What you see below is the result of several attempts to re-work an old statement.

Permission-giving statement #1

"Everyone uses credit, it's part of life."

Attempt# 1 "Credit is part of life, and everyone uses it."

Attempt#2 "Credit is part of life, maybe not everyone uses it."

Attempt #3 "Credit is part of people's lives, and it's a choice, although it doesn't feel like it."

Attempt#4 "I don't want credit to be running my life, so I will have to choose differently."

Attempt #5 "There is credit if I need it, and I'd rather not use it."

Final motivator statement:

Credit is available, but I have found that it complicates my life and I want to use it less or not at all.

Here are other examples of re-working permission-giving statements:

Permission-giving statement: "Being in debt is part of life."

Motivator statement: I can save for most things I

need.

Permission-giving statement: "Everyone I know has credit."

Motivator statement: Whatever others do, I want to be in control of my finances.

Permission-giving statement: "I can pay the minimum and everything will be fine."

Motivator statement: Paying the minimum just keeps me in debt and stressed out.

Permission-giving statement: "I'll pay it off next month."

Motivator statement: Although I'd like to, I rarely pay off my credit cards and my debt load just increases, so I'll be careful about when I use credit.

Permission-giving statement: "Who can save without using credit?"

Motivator statement: It's possible to save for things I really need.

These motivator statements are balanced, open to possibilities, more flexible and less rigid. Motivator statements really come into their own when you:

1. Repeat them to integrate them into your thinking and,

2. Practice using them when you are triggered to spend in your problematic spending areas.

Why Motivator statements work:

- They create doubt when you want to use the old permission-giving statements.

- They are factual, positive and based in reality.

- They help you to experience a sense of control in your life.

Permission-giving statements de-motivate you. Motivating statements are just that, motivating.

By re-working the phrase,

"Who can save without using credit?" to

"It's possible to save for things I really need," you are actually doubting what you used to say to yourself. The motivator statement forces a pause between thought and behavior. Motivator affirmations then become guidelines for the new actions we are striving for.

Sharon's Motivators:

~ I have a right to be curious about others' needs, rather than respond to my assumptions.

~ I cannot presume to know what makes my husband happy.

~ I have a right to question and to disagree with my husband about what my money is spent on.

~ I like camping, and I would also like to do other things with my family that don't cost money.

~ I need boundaries around the line of credit.

~ I can choose to go or not go gambling.

Re-working permission-giving statements can at times feel clumsy or forced. You may find yourself arguing with your new Motivator statements. However, Sharon experienced how powerful they can be when her behavior began to change. She began to hesitate and question herself before going gambling. Over time, Sharon's Motivator statements undermined her enjoyment of gambling, and she gambled less and less. She decided to self-exclude from the casino and stopped gambling. Her Motivator statements gave Sharon a sense of control and increased self-esteem and she pushed herself to discuss finances with her husband, and to talk about her needs. She made a list of family activities that were free or nearly free in and around their community for the family to do together. Sharon usually experienced fear in bringing up money with her husband. He was the assertive one she had believed. Her new statements provided impetus to practice assertiveness skills with him.

Bob's Motivators

~ I would like to help my mother, but not have her totally dependent on me.

~ I like to take care of my family, and it's OK to say no to some of the expenses.

~ I can find other ways to relax, not just by using alcohol.

Bob was surprised at how much guilt played a role in his life and in his spending. Guilt spending means that the person often doesn't question what or why they are spending on others. Bob felt guilty or bad for others. He told himself that he didn't 'care', but in truth his resentment was emerging in other ways, such as being snappy with his colleagues, or grumpy with his children. He then felt guilty about his behavior; guilt trapping him even more. It is natural to feel resentment if we are giving too much. Bob later questioned whether this underlying resentment sometimes fueled his alcohol use, which he knew Trish wasn't happy about.

Bob learned that he had other feelings too. His challenge was to pay attention to when he did things out of guilt. Guilt had hijacked his life, and Bob wanted to determine his life in a more conscious way. Like many of my clients, Bob was amazed to see how many of his actions were promoted by his set of permission-giving statements and that he could change them. He became quite excited to see what life was going to offer.

Over time, Bob noticed that his relationships with his family felt different. He avoided conversations less and asked more questions instead of being silent in many social interactions. He felt more confident and a little more present. He experienced new energy and an interest in the family finances. He devised a system whereby each person in the family had their own shoebox, into which they would put all their receipts. This included his children. Bob wanted his children to learn about their spending habits and wanted to know their thoughts and feelings. The family began to meet and to discuss their needs, and their desires.

For the first time in his life, Bob started to think about what he wanted to do, too. He started to go to the local Rec center and joined a swim and weight class. Importantly, he began to have discussions with his mother. In these discussions, he noticed that he talked more about himself, and some of his limits, including his financial limits. They had to figure out what his mother was going to do with her living expenses. Eventually, his mother moved into an apartment and Bob and Trish set a limit of money they could afford to give to her to offset her expenses.

Bob and Trish decided to cut back on some of the children's sporting activities, as they were spending another $350.00 a month they couldn't truly afford. Both Bob and Trish had decided that they had to make their future retirement something achievable.

Because Bob had focused on reducing his guilt spending, he found that he actually had some extra money after paying bills at the end of the month, the first time since he had started working. He noticed that he felt less stressed, and that he and Trish had improved their communication. Over time, his depression lifted. We continued to discuss his feelings about his mother, and Bob experienced a lightening of his guilt. Through discussion and reflection, Bob saw that his mother had a tendency to lay some guilt on him. He worked on detaching from that guilt, (using Step 4 to create a factual statement list and permission-giving statement list about guilt), and on spending time with his mother that didn't relate to helping her.

Lorna's Motivators:

~ Liesa is capable in some parts of her life, and she can grow to be more capable.

~ Rory is responsible for making his life better.

~ Food represents one part of my life, and I

can get solace and peace from other things.

Lorna's guilt spending had imperiled her present and future. She had been afraid for years that if she said no to her children that she would alienate them. Lorna acknowledged that she was deeply lonely, and that solving her children's problems gave her purpose.

Detaching emotionally from what you see on the paper can be very challenging, as you are evaluating what you see based on what you *used* to think. Sometimes it's helpful to talk with others about what they see. The people that we regularly turn to can be helpful to us; but assess this carefully. Asking others to help us, when they have a vested interest in us staying the same may not be the best choice.

Lorna had this experience when she started to talk to her children about what she wanted to do differently. In fact, some of her fears about being alienated from her children became reality for a period of time. When we talk to people about what we are trying to do, we can be overtly or covertly asking their permission. If we *act rather than talk about* what is in our best interests, those around us will *have* to act differently. This lessens the need for lengthy conversations about what you need from them, which likely hasn't gotten you anywhere before.

"I tried talking to my daughter about what I wanted, but she got really upset with me, and started to blame me for all of her problems. Each time I addressed her behavior, the conversation became more about her and her needs than mine. I can see that based on my behaviors around money and my children, it seems to me that I often feel guilty and much of my present spending on them is related to that feeling. It's true though, that they know how to make me feel guilty too! I will drop everything for them.

"I believed that I can't say no, or that I have to say yes so I don't disappoint them. I worry about them. I tell myself that I'm not a good parent because my children are struggling emotionally and financially in their lives. I can see now that I blame myself wholly for that. When I was growing up, I couldn't say no. I was expected to help, to be there for everyone all the time, as a kind of replacement mother. And so, being a mother from the time I was very young, my beliefs around money must have developed from that. What I had I had to share. I wasn't allowed to have any extra money of my own. Of course, growing up, I didn't hear people talk about money, about the importance of saving or anything like that. It was more about survival. I don't just want to survive now, I want to thrive."

Lorna's need to overspend money on her children was promoted by guilt and obligated spending, as she suffered from the 'I should haves'.

Thorny emotional issues can seem, in hindsight, to be obvious. However, we have to watch that we don't judge ourselves or others. Lorna could now adjust her spending based on her Motivator Statements. These were her new guidelines, reminding her that she needed limits to what she spent on her children, and that she had a right to say no to pressure from them. Lorna noticed that she began to feel less guilty. She was experiencing life more authentically. She interacted with her children differently, steering conversations toward helping them to see options, rather than to look to her to help them out. She reported, somewhat gleefully, during this time that she didn't take a phone call from her son, a first for her, while she was at her book club meeting. Prior to that she would always immediately take the call, increasing her anxiety, as well as setting herself up as the crisis manager of her children's lives.

Working with her new behavior guidelines helped Lorna set better boundaries with her children, and, helped her to focus on building her own life, apart from them. She'd always wanted to take painting classes. The Steps had assisted her in saving towards those classes. Of course, it would take time to wean her children off of their over-reliance on their mother and her over-focus on them. Occasionally Lorna would slip into her old role as savior. However, as time went on, and she practiced her Motivators, she began to feel uncomfortable with the savior role and her behavior reflected her new way of thinking and feeling.

Wendy's Motivators:

If emotional needs are not sufficiently met at critical times, it is difficult to then have the skills to meet those needs as an adult.

Of course, given that we are emotional animals, there will always be times in our lives when our emotional needs aren't met as our caregivers cannot be 100% emotionally attuned to us at all times. However, in some families, there is very little emotional attunement to our needs, leaving lasting wounds.

Wendy had had a particularly insufficient childhood. She was caught in a cycle of loneliness, which was bolstered by an inability to reach out and connect with others. The only emotional connection she experienced within herself was when she shopped. In those moments Wendy experienced some control and a release of emotions. I encouraged her to develop only one Motivator Statement to take her forward, to keep her emotional distress to a minimum in the initial phases of integrating the Steps.

"I can learn to connect with others."

The therapeutic relationship provides a format to practice new skills. Especially important for those learning how to connect emotionally with others. To feel connected to others takes a number of steps. As Wendy had low self-esteem, she isolated from others by working long hours and keeping to herself in her personal life. As she was isolated, with very little social integration, she rarely experienced others' interest or care. Her belief that she was unlovable was never tested and her cycle of isolation continued. Her lack of social connection enabled the addiction to spending when depressed to flourish. To start the healing process, Wendy had to contextualize her childhood and adult experiences.

How to contextualize: I did X, because of Y, and I learned to Z because of that experience

---

This healing tool is *different* to rehashing the past. When we acknowledge ourselves and our difficult experiences, we enable our true feelings to surface.

To deepen healing, name the feeling as it arises. For example, "I am feeling sad right now because of X". We can also write this feeling down. The emotion is then released from us. Some experiences have feelings that are so strongly attached to them, that we may have to repeat this exercise over and over until we begin to feel some relief from the feelings' intensity. This is a wellness practice for our entire lifetimes.

Slowly, Wendy began to feel better and spend less impulsively. Over the next few months, she read books on self-esteem and attended a group on that topic. It was very helpful for Wendy to hear that there were many other people who experienced life as she did.

Wendy also set some new boundaries with her family. Conversations with family members often became unhelpful to her. She would start the conversation, ever hopeful that her emotional needs would be met, and end the conversation hurting more. I encouraged Wendy to move the topic of conversation back onto her family member, to have shorter check-ins, versus longer conversations, which would inevitably turn into criticisms of Wendy. Wendy literally timed her conversations and would end them under five minutes. Wendy reported feeling better about these conversations as a sense of control developed.

Mary's Motivators:

- ~ I want all of my significant relationships to improve.
- ~ I have to keep money for my future.
- ~ I am at the center of my life; I cannot make

someone else the center of my life.

~ I've done my best with Harris, but all the money I've given him hasn't changed anything.

Mary began to see Harris in a different light. Rather than attributing all of his behavior and choices to her, she saw that he had choices to make too, and that he tended to procrastinate and blame others for his problems. He was also quick to use others. Mary couldn't do all that needed to done by herself. She and her husband entered couples counselling for a period of time as she wanted to make amends to Ed. She wanted her marriage to work and their relationship had felt strained for some time. Her husband Ed had been hurt by Mary's focus on Harris. In response, Ed had pulled back and become critical of Mary, something he had to stop.

There wasn't any point in rehashing what could have been. However, much could be gained by focusing on "what now?" Negotiating a new pattern of behavior with Harris was the next step. They decided to make decisions around money and Harris together. This helped Mary to alter her automatic response of simply giving money to Harris. In a way, giving Harris money distanced her from him. They were often at loggerheads despite the money, as Mary felt resentful and Harris felt put upon by life.

Harris was practiced at separating Mary from Ed and applying pressure for money. So, when they decided to always talk to Harris about money together, the pressure was borne by both of them. Initially, Harris didn't like the new regime and found ways to pressure Mary when he knew Ed wasn't around. Mostly, Mary stuck to her new behavior by saying that she ~ould talk to Harris when Ed was available. Harris distanced himself from her which was hurtful. However, Mary focused on her vision of the future. Bearing the hurt, and continuing to present a united front to Harris, was a powerful tool which paid off over time.

Carol's Motivators:

~ Sharing my negative emotions will help me not to shop when I'm feeling lonely.

~ I will work towards eradicating debt, and I can live debt free.

~ I am allowed to ask for help when I don't know the answers.

~ I can share all parts of me with my husband, and this is important to do so for our relationship.

Embedded in these statements are the actions that Carol had to implement. She decided to sign up for a course in communications as she struggled to find the words to describe her life to others. She consulted a financial planner to determine a way out of her debt. She and her husband decided to go for couples counselling, to learn more loving and effective communication. Carol's husband too, struggled to assert himself in their relationship and had acknowledged to Carol that he felt lonely. By sharing their true feelings, Carol said she felt closer to her husband and he to her.

Your new motivating statements will, over time, become the new foundation of who you are becoming.

It will take time to discover all of the permission-giving statements that you have in each problematic spending area. So that you don't become overwhelmed, start with re-working one or two permission-giving statements, and then practice your new Motivators. If you see that your behavior starts to wander back to the old ways, review your list, to see if there are some other permission-giving statements that you need to re-work.

Our permission-giving statements have become foundational to who we are; we could say that they form part of our belief system. With the application of the 5 steps, you therefore are altering parts of your beliefs that do not work for you, in a clear step by step fashion. By practicing your Motivator Statements in real life situations, you will see whether your statements are strong enough, and, whether you might have missed a permission-giving statement that needs re-working. And, as with Sharon, Bob, Lorna, Carol, Wendy and Mary, your life will alter in myriad of ways. If all of your life is interconnected, then altering one part of your life positively, will affect the other parts of your life in positive ways too.

Action Step after completing Step 4.

To help you remember your Motivator Statements, write your Motivator Statements on a card and carry them with you, or make a voice memo on your smartphone.

Chapter Six:
Step 5: E is for Experience - Create the most abundant life you can

Now that you are at your 5th step, you might notice yourself catching your permission-giving statements sooner. Your beliefs about yourself may be altering. Beliefs about who we are, how we are supposed to behave, and even what we like or don't like are also constructed by our interactions with ourselves and others. Beliefs about money are ingrained by the time we start spending, and we rarely look at them again, until perhaps, we have to. As we have seen, when emotional wounds direct our spending, we can also be certain that emotional wounds will have had a part in constructing our belief system about who we are and how we *should* behave.

Over time, beliefs tend to become black and white and rigid. The 5 Step Plan unlocks your potential for you to actively change your beliefs, and, increases your flexibility and creativity.

Without attention, silver tarnishes. Like silver, our emotional work must and can be polished. I wish we could polish once; and be all shiny. However, like silver, we need to polish ourselves again and again. Our emotional tarnishing usually comes from unsatisfactory interactions with those around us. A useful emotional tool is to view even unsatisfactory interactions as ways to polish internally. People will directly or indirectly, help us to polish ourselves. By reflecting, drawing on the tools in this book and learning from others, you can practice the 5 Steps. Daily reflection and polishing in small ways helps to prepare for those larger painful tarnishing actions from others. Any polishing is good polishing. Don't wait for the big change moments; acknowledge and celebrate any positive change within yourself.

Your abundant life is supported by having control. A sense of inner control helps us all to feel happier. The journey through the 5 Step Plan took you through your personal, unique story to gain understanding about who you are, and why parts of your life have unfolded as they have. Steps 2 to 4 helped to deepen and expand your self-esteem with self-knowledge. This is true power: the power to change parts of your life that don't work the way you wish them to, the self-confidence to follow your wishes through, and more money to enable more choices.

Now you can alter your life course to create the abundant life that you desire. When interlocking behaviors alter and change, the shape of your life has to change accordingly. Your internal life will meet your external life differently over time. This is not a process that can be hurried, as change will resist attempts to speed it up. You could miss the subtle nuances of change, and you won't have the experience of enjoying the evolution of you.

Create a collage of how your new life will unfold, incorporating your Motivator Statements.

An abundant life can be anything you choose. For some, it is time to expand and develop hobbies, for others it may be finding a way of giving back or of focusing on building a supportive network of people. The point is that giving yourself power to determine more of your choices is luscious payment for all of your hard work in the previous Steps.

I'm sure you've already realized that each of our narrators experienced their abundance differently; however, to enjoy their successes will not be to compare each person's choices or compare them to yours. This is your time to be the creative artist in your own life, determining your own path.

Sharon

"I am a different person today," Sharon said, some months after our initial meeting, "I actually said no to my husband!" Sharon laughed, and she looked considerably younger than her 45 years. "I feel like I have different relationships within my family," she said, "my children appear to respect me more and they ask for less. My husband takes my opinion into account, and I listen to my own gut now, in a way that I didn't before." Sharon eventually shared her gambling problem with her husband. Initially he had struggled to understand and be supportive of her. However, after many discussions they were

81

able to work through this challenge "I've had to stand up for myself in that too," said Sharon. "He had to realize that I wasn't perfect, that I too can and do make mistakes. Just like him." Sharon had decided to take a break from her dental assistant job for a time, to re-work her home life, and to spend more time with her children in a different way than staged trips away. She had been able to cut down on their grocery bill, making food that was less expensive. The family had also decided to cut back on the trips to see family who lived out of town. Sharon had invited her family to visit her. Sharon didn't immediately eradicate her gambling, which was her goal. However, over time, her gambling sessions became less and less and she spent less money doing so. Sharon was enjoying her life in a way that she hadn't experienced in a long, long time.

Bob

"I find I can give to myself now, rather than just every-one around me," said Bob. "At first this seemed very selfish, and I doubted myself all the time. You and I dis-cussed the importance of giving to myself many times too," Bob intoned. "I think that questioning is part of this, going back over decisions and seeing the links over and over again. It's opened up a new world for me." Bob was smiling ear to ear. "Trish and I have a fi-nancial plan now, one that sees me retiring when I'm 66. I've had time to really concentrate on my health, and my heart function is so much better. Colleagues seem to like me more, and some ask for my help, which never happened before, I think they were scared of me.
"My last employee performance report was good actually. I think I've settled into the idea of working until just past 66, giving me a goal that's clear. Trish and I seem able to talk more easily too, and our

relationship seems closer. It's not all roses of course. She still tells me that I keep stuff back and I try to speak up more, but I'm still scared of creating conflict. That conflict resolution course you referred me to really helped though, gave me food for thought. Life feels good now."

Lorna

"I think I actually like my children more now," said Lorna. "They've stopped asking me for money all the time. I realize now how much annoyance I constantly had and felt trapped to help them. I was so o-b-l-i-g-a-t-e-d," said Lorna stressing every letter. "It was so tiring emotionally, I just couldn't focus on me at all. I am really trying to get my eating under control too now. I can see clearly that I eat when stressed. I obviously like food," she said patting her diminishing middle, "but I've realized that I can have control there too. I've joined a fitness club with a friend and we cheer each other on. I'm having fun. I never had fun before.

"Life feels richer somehow. And I do have more money. This same friend and I, are planning a trip to Greece. I'm going to need a couple of years to save up for it, but I'm going to do it. After I pay off my credit card!" Lorna laughed. "Yes, I know what you'd say if I didn't." I nodded, smiling in agreement. Lorna was anticipating my reactions accurately.

Mary

Mary's relationship with Harris remained tense for some time. She had to fight feelings of sadness and anxiety about his future. However, Mary was gaining support for the changes she was making from family and friends. "I can see I've been difficult to deal with," Mary said ruefully, "I was so defensive all the time. No one could tell me anything. I know that started when I was a child and continued on into adulthood. I've realized that I've lost friends over Harris and my stubbornness. The other day, even Harris told me I'm stubborn, although I think he was referring to me not helping him out." Mary paused. "I prefer to call that assertiveness!"

Over two years had passed since Mary and I had initially met. During that time, Mary limited what money she gave to Harris, improved her relationship with her husband, friends and family, and even took a trip with her husband, leaving Harris at home. "I've begun to realize that Harris has real problems fitting into the real world," said Mary during one of our conversations. "Honestly, I think I've made that worse for him, as I am not sure if Harris can make it on his own." Mary and her husband decided to maintain the status quo, with Harris remaining living in their basement, but having him participate more in family times, as it was clear that Harris was not a typical boomerang child. Harris was very isolated socially and reliant on Mary. Mary organized outreach counselling for Harris, to take some of the pressure off of her.

Although Harris initially resisted this idea, Mary gently insisted over time, and Harris eventually agreed. "I told him that I was too stressed to continue the way things were," said Mary. "Maybe that was good, because Harris can now think of someone besides himself. I have more time for myself, I have a little more money in my account and life feels so much better now."

Wendy

Wendy's transformation was truly remarkable. Through her application of the 5 Step Plan, a self-esteem course and taking kayaking lessons, Wendy's life changed completely. Her spending on 'stuff' dwindled and she was able to buy herself kayak equipment. She joined a local club and began to be invited to events related to kayaking. She met and befriended a woman around her age and the two of them became best friends.

Wendy had never been able to emotionally connect fully with another adult and this relationship was instrumental in helping her to blossom. Her fitness improved along with her self-esteem. During calls with her mother, she was able to talk about something beyond work.

Although her mother continued to pester her about "a relationship," Wendy was also able to stand up for herself and told her mother to stop asking her. "I told her that I'm not interested right now; that I'm working on myself. How can I offer anyone anything right now, and mother asking only makes me feel worse about being single!"

This was one of many turning points that Wendy experienced. Wendy was aware that her life was suffering due to the amount of time that work took up. Although scared, she stopped taking work home. "I truly do think I've lost career momentum by not working lots of overtime like the rest of my colleagues; I don't want to get to the end of my life and all I've got to show for it is a whole lot of reports with my name attached." Wendy laughed. I commented on how wonderful it was to hear her laugh. "I didn't laugh much before, but I do now."

As if she was proving that point, Wendy chuckled. This time at herself. "I was so stuck!" she said. Using gentle humor, Wendy was demonstrating a powerful emotional technique which helps to free us from self-judgment and criticism. "I'm really living now," Wendy said, "and I don't want to stop."

Carol

At the year mark after our initial meeting, Carol's financial life looked quite different. "I'm not stressed about money like I was. Understanding my problematic spending behaviors and altering them has made such a big difference. I decided to pay off the debt with my husband's help, and work towards spending differently. We agreed that we needed to make friends. I had no idea that I was so isolated and spending so much time fiddling with our finances. I also didn't know how supportive Greg could be. This whole process has renewed our relationship together. I'm so grateful. I didn't know how stuck I was in the patterns of my childhood and how that was creating such a diminished life.

"Today, life truly does feel abundant, and I have so much more energy to give to others and Greg. I always believed that Greg was unable to talk so I held back from him. But in reality, he was holding back because he thought that's what I wanted. He didn't want to push me away any further so he was always careful, too careful to upset me. He's begun to challenge me. It's still a surprise when he tells me how he feels. Truthfully sometimes I don't really want to hear about it, but I know that our communication is so much better."

Chapter Seven:
Imagining Your Plan

Abundance comes in many different forms. Being able to be present, in your life and in others' lives naturally imbues your life with a richness that money cannot buy. Knowledge of the intricacies of life and trusting that things will work out will become more available to you. Solving emotional issues helps to raise serotonin and dopamine levels, and a new curiosity about how your life will unfold will develop. With more time to delve into life, interests and hobbies, connections can and do present themselves to you. Try saying no, instead of yes, and yes instead of no. Play with your automatic responses.

Journaling is a wonderful way to review and track progress. Each day can be a way to ask yourself, "Am I spending this day wisely? Do I feel freer?" Continue to work with your fears and concerns compassionately. Some days will be gold, and others like stone, yet the days will pass, no matter whether we are enjoying them or not, feel like we've been ripped off, or take out our frustrations on those around us. Work towards squeezing the best out of your life, every day.

There are literally hundreds of interesting hobbies or interests to try. Turn your hobby into income, try a new interest, check in with your local library for groups to join, volunteer for something you are passionate about, read the books you've always wanted to, start a course, offer a course or go to school. Adopting the attitude of a lifelong learner about the world around you and about your own inner world will pay you real dividends.

You can use the 5 Step Plan in all areas of your life. There are always resistances within us, behaviors that we wish we could change. Instead of struggling in your relationship with money, you now have the emotional space and time to polish the work of art that is you. There is no creature on earth like you, and no one that follows will be the same. Each time you interact with yourself and with others, you have an opportunity to show others all the hard work and polishing you have done.

With your bank balance reflecting your new-found inner abundance, enjoy the journey. There are no destinations, only adventures.

Suggested Reading

Brown, Edward Espe (1997) *Tomato Blessings and Radish Teachings*. Riverhead Books.

Dyer, Frank (2011) The Annotated AA Handbook. A Companion to the Big Book. Barricade Books.

Chimsky, Mark, Editor (2012) *65 Things to Do When You Retire*. Sellers Publishing Inc.

Davis, Martha, Robbins Eshelman, Elizabeth and McKay Matthew (1988). *The Relaxation and Stress Reduction Workbook.* New Harbinger Publications.

Eisler, Riane (2008) *The Real Wealth of Nations*. Boerett-Koehler Publishers.

Ellis, Albert. (1994). *Reason and Emotion in Psychotherapy*. NY: Birch Lane Press

Ferriss, Timothy (2007). *The 4-Hour Workweek*. Crown Publishing.

Goleman, Daniel (2006) Emotional Intelligence, why it can matter more than IQ. Bantam Books.

Karmarkar, U. R., Shiv, B., Knutson, B. (2014) "Cost conscious? The neural and behavioral impact of price primacy on decision making." Journal of Marketing Research.

Robin, Vicki and Dominguez, Joe (1992). *Your Money or Your Life*. Penguin Books.

Lerner, Jennifer (2015). "Annual Review of Psychology" 66:33.1-33.25.

Mate, Gabor (2008*). In the Realm of the Hungry Ghosts*. North Atlantic Books.

Matthews, A. M (2000). *The Seven Keys to Calm.* Penguin Press.

Ruiz, Miguel and Ruiz, José Louis (2010). *The Fifth Agreement.* Amber-Allen Publishing.

Vaz-Oxlade, Gail (2009). *Debt-Free Forever.* Collins.

Yeager, Jeff (2013). *How to Retire the Cheapskate Way.* Three Rivers Press.

Contact me via

http://jennifermannauthor.com

Jennifer.mann.ca@gmail.com

jennifer@jennifermannauthor.com

Notes

Notes

Notes

Notes

Made in the USA
Columbia, SC
02 September 2018